About Skill Builders Math

by Carolyn Chapman

Welcome to RBP Books' Skill Builders series. Like our Summer Bridge Activities collection, the Skill Builders series is designed to make learning both fun and rewarding.

Skill Builders 5th Grade Math provides students with focused practice to help them reinforce and develop math skills. Each Skill Builders volume is grade-level appropriate, with clear examples and instructions to guide each lesson. In accordance with NCTM standards, exercises for grade five cover a variety of math skills, including addition, subtraction, multiplication, division, word problems, geometry, graphing, money values, fractions, and decimals.

A critical thinking section includes exercises to help develop higher-order thinking skills.

Learning is more effective when approached with an element of fun and enthusiasm—just as most children approach life. That's why the Skill Builders combine entertaining and academically sound exercises and fun themes to make reviewing basic skills fun and effective, for both you and your budding scholars.

Table of Contents

State Stats

Sam is studying U.S. states in his geography class. The chart below shows the area for different states. Help him complete the chart. The first one is done for you.

Place	Area in Square Miles	Rounded to Thousands	Rounded to Hundreds
Alabama	52,419	52,000	52,400
Alaska	663,267		
California	163,696		
Delaware	2,489		
Georgia	59,425		
Kansas	82,277		
Maryland	12,407		
Mississippi	48,430		
Nevada	110,561		
New York	54,556		
Oregon	98,381		
Rhode Island	1,545		
Texas	268,581		
Wyoming	97,814		

Math Grade 5—RBP0040

Write the number that means the same as the following:

1. 50,000 + 2,000 + 500 + 70 + 6

2. 20,000 + 6,000 + 900 + 10 + 5

3. 30,000 + 8,000 + 500 + 10 + 5

4. 430,000 + 4,000 + 600 + 20 + 9

5. 960,000 + 8,000 + 300 + 30 + 1

6. 640,000 + 20,000 + 100 + 80 + 2

7. 850,000 + 80,000 + 3,000 + 500 + 7

8. 300,000 + 6,000 + 100 + 30 + 2

9. 710,000 + 1,000 + 300 + 60 + 1

10. 450,000 + 7,000 + 200 + 20 + 9

11. 200,000 + 3,000 + 800 + 70 + 4

2

Write the number that means the same as the following:

1. 7 hundreds, 3 tens, and 1 one

2. 34 thousands, 7 hundreds, 3 tens, and 0 ones

3. 60 thousands, 2 hundreds, 7 tens, and 3 ones

4. 2 hundreds, 6 tens, and 4 ones

5. 27 thousands, 6 hundreds, 9 tens, and 4 ones

6. 16 thousands, 7 hundreds, 9 tens, and 2 ones

7. 89 thousands, 4 hundreds, 6 tens, and 3 ones

8. 5 hundreds, 8 tens, and 9 ones

9. 36 thousands, 8 hundreds, 3 tens, and 5 ones

10. 230 thousands, 5 hundreds, 8 tens, and 9 ones

11. 4 hundreds, 6 tens, and 5 ones

Find the sum for each problem.

1.

176	945	709	406
+ 549	+ 754	+ 665	+ 186
725			

2.

3,571	2,701	4,855	9,423
+ 1,853	+ 8,194	+ 6,806	+ 3,750

3.

36,761	79,246	43,751	85,243
+ 74,485	+ 51,184	+ 67,169	+ 13,267

4.

464	161	468	991
653	363	616	597
+ 444	+ 186	+ 787	+ 227

5.

6,254	8,644	7,423	6,064
5,401	2,645	8,531	4,008
4,674	2,752	1,754	7,640
+ 3,125	+ 1,660	+ 4,405	+ 1,028

RememBer... Include the comma in your answer!

Solve each problem.

1.

$$
\begin{array}{r}
{\scriptstyle 1} \\
5,136 \\
+\,2,549 \\
\hline
\mathbf{7,685}
\end{array}
\qquad
\begin{array}{r}
3,453 \\
+\,7,465 \\
\hline
\end{array}
\qquad
\begin{array}{r}
7,432 \\
+\,2,386 \\
\hline
\end{array}
\qquad
\begin{array}{r}
2,973 \\
+\,2,753 \\
\hline
\end{array}
$$

2.

$$
\begin{array}{r}
74,531 \\
+\,30,593 \\
\hline
\end{array}
\qquad
\begin{array}{r}
15,472 \\
+\,40,765 \\
\hline
\end{array}
\qquad
\begin{array}{r}
66,734 \\
+\,18,139 \\
\hline
\end{array}
\qquad
\begin{array}{r}
57,440 \\
+\,11,679 \\
\hline
\end{array}
$$

3.

$$
\begin{array}{r}
915,341 \\
+\,65,433 \\
\hline
\end{array}
\qquad
\begin{array}{r}
103,256 \\
+\,67,525 \\
\hline
\end{array}
\qquad
\begin{array}{r}
545,971 \\
+\,31,716 \\
\hline
\end{array}
\qquad
\begin{array}{r}
673,665 \\
+\,41,698 \\
\hline
\end{array}
$$

4.

$$
\begin{array}{r}
435,467 \\
+\,674,577 \\
\hline
\end{array}
\qquad
\begin{array}{r}
933,845 \\
+\,127,747 \\
\hline
\end{array}
\qquad
\begin{array}{r}
893,863 \\
+\,953,523 \\
\hline
\end{array}
\qquad
\begin{array}{r}
456,768 \\
+\,854,127 \\
\hline
\end{array}
$$

5.

$$
\begin{array}{r}
5,656 \\
8,656 \\
3,642 \\
+\,1,599 \\
\hline
\end{array}
\qquad
\begin{array}{r}
9,003 \\
5,855 \\
9,673 \\
+\,3,794 \\
\hline
\end{array}
\qquad
\begin{array}{r}
5,567 \\
1,355 \\
2,078 \\
+\,5,853 \\
\hline
\end{array}
\qquad
\begin{array}{r}
6,742 \\
2,153 \\
9,432 \\
+\,4,117 \\
\hline
\end{array}
$$

Put the correct sign (>, <, =) in each equation.

1. 54,233 $>$ 54,203

2. 17,021 $\bigcirc$ 17,210

3. 643 $\bigcirc$ 463

4. 632,972 $\bigcirc$ 623,792

5. 41,101 $\bigcirc$ 41,001

6. 864,916 $\bigcirc$ 864,619

7. 34,400 $\bigcirc$ 34,400

8. 6,729 $\bigcirc$ 6,927

9. 454,680 $\bigcirc$ 454,086

10. 101,000 $\bigcirc$ 110,000

11. 909,464 $\bigcirc$ 909,644

12. 31,001 $\bigcirc$ 31,101

13. 7,579 $\bigcirc$ 7,579

14. 879,301 $\bigcirc$ 879,031

15. 85,101 $\bigcirc$ 85,001

16. 609,766 $\bigcirc$ 609,676

17. 407,101 $\bigcirc$ 409,101

18. 94,201 $\bigcirc$ 94,201

Solve each problem.

1.

$$\begin{array}{r} {}^{4}\!{}^{12}\!{}^{1}\!5\cancel{3}2 \\ -\ 165 \\ \hline \mathbf{367} \end{array}$$

$$\begin{array}{r} 648 \\ -\ 497 \\ \hline \end{array}$$

$$\begin{array}{r} 354 \\ -\ 285 \\ \hline \end{array}$$

$$\begin{array}{r} 674 \\ -\ 158 \\ \hline \end{array}$$

2.

$$\begin{array}{r} 101 \\ -\ 67 \\ \hline \end{array}$$

$$\begin{array}{r} 256 \\ -\ 148 \\ \hline \end{array}$$

$$\begin{array}{r} 765 \\ -\ 378 \\ \hline \end{array}$$

$$\begin{array}{r} 923 \\ -\ 658 \\ \hline \end{array}$$

3.

$$\begin{array}{r} 854 \\ -\ 169 \\ \hline \end{array}$$

$$\begin{array}{r} 773 \\ -\ 487 \\ \hline \end{array}$$

$$\begin{array}{r} 544 \\ -\ 375 \\ \hline \end{array}$$

$$\begin{array}{r} 634 \\ -\ 479 \\ \hline \end{array}$$

4.

$$\begin{array}{r} 4{,}551 \\ -\ 2{,}957 \\ \hline \end{array}$$

$$\begin{array}{r} 7{,}452 \\ -\ 3{,}284 \\ \hline \end{array}$$

$$\begin{array}{r} 1{,}531 \\ -\ 1{,}368 \\ \hline \end{array}$$

$$\begin{array}{r} 8{,}451 \\ -\ 4{,}276 \\ \hline \end{array}$$

5.

$$\begin{array}{r} 7{,}681 \\ -\ 5{,}099 \\ \hline \end{array}$$

$$\begin{array}{r} 3{,}002 \\ -\ 1{,}698 \\ \hline \end{array}$$

$$\begin{array}{r} 7{,}515 \\ -\ 2{,}907 \\ \hline \end{array}$$

$$\begin{array}{r} 9{,}461 \\ -\ 2{,}576 \\ \hline \end{array}$$

Remember... Include the comma in your answer!

Solve each problem.

1.	984 − 487	435 − 279	381 − 179	674 − 467
2.	374 − 87	757 − 569	673 − 194	734 − 355
3.	108 − 29	780 − 176	582 − 354	845 − 165
4.	4,762 − 2,268	3,642 − 1,286	9,003 − 4,357	7,041 − 2,353
5.	64,546 − 8,349	90,442 − 6,346	15,753 − 2,657	75,604 − 23,892

Heather and her friends are shopping at the grocery store. Round each item to the nearest dollar. Use the prices and estimate the amount of each shopping list.

$.89 $2.63 $1.89 $2.57 $7.58 $2.09 $2.63 $4.35 $1.37 $1.15

1. Gary's shopping list: bananas, 2 bags of sugar, cereal, and soda
$1.00 + $3.00 + $3.00 + $4.00 + $2.00 = $13.00

2. Amber's shopping list: 3 loaves of bread, milk, and eggs

3. Jean's shopping list: jam, flour, and cheese

4. Heather's shopping list: 2 bags of flour, milk, and 4 boxes of cereal

5. Jack's shopping list: soda and 3 packages of cereal

6. Emma's shopping list: 2 cartons of eggs, cheese, and soda

7. Anne's shopping list: 3 loaves of bread and 2 bottles of jam

8. Dexter's shopping list: sugar, 2 cartons of milk, and cheese

Math Grade 5—RBP0040

Now figure the actual cost for each list of groceries.

1. Gary's shopping list: bananas, 2 bags of sugar, cereal, and soda

2. Amber's shopping list: 3 loaves of bread, milk, and eggs

3. Jean's shopping list: jam, flour, and cheese

4. Heather's shopping list: 2 bags of flour, milk, and 4 boxes of cereal

5. Jack's shopping list: soda and 3 packages of cereal

6. Emma's shopping list: 2 cartons of eggs, cheese, and soda

7. Anne's shopping list: 3 loaves of bread and 2 bottles of jam

8. Dexter's shopping list: sugar, 2 cartons of milk, and cheese

Plot the points on the coordinate system graph. The first number is how far across. The second number is how far up or down.

1. (5, 3)

2. (–4, –2)

3. (3, 2)

4. (0, –4)

5. (–4, 1)

6. (2, –3)

7. (2, –1)

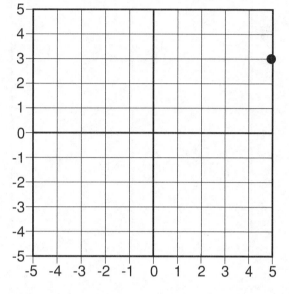

Use the coordinate system below to fill in the missing points.

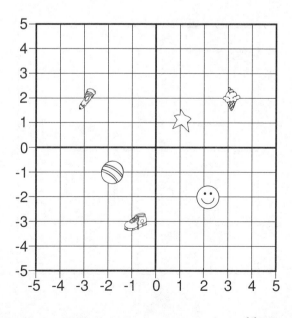

8. ____, ____

9. ☺ ____, ____

10. 🍦 ____, ____

11. ☆ ____, ____

12. ◉ ____, ____

13. ✏ ____, ____

Use the coordinate system below to fill in the missing points.

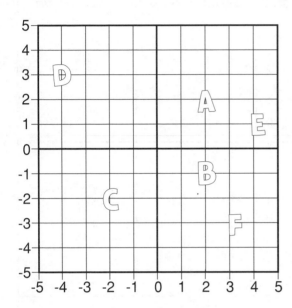

1. A ___, ___

2. B ___, ___

3. C ___, ___

4. D ___, ___

5. E ___, ___

6. F ___, ___

Plot the points on the graph below.

7. (−1, 4)

8. (5, 4)

9. (0, −2)

10. (−3, 1)

11. (3, 3)

12. (−4, −5)

13. (2, −3)

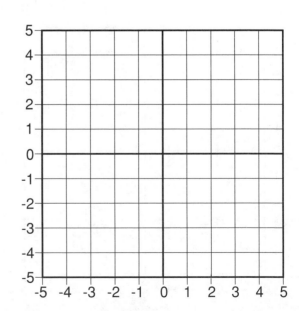

12

Perimeter Projects

Find the perimeter of each shape below.

Remember... The **perimeter** is the distance around a figure. To find the perimeter of a figure, add up the lengths of each side of the figure.

1.

16 m

8 m

2.

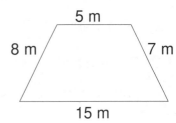

5 m

8 m   7 m

15 m

3.

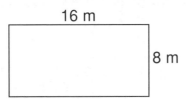

9 in.

9 in.

4.

24 cm

13 cm

5.

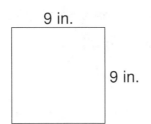

13 m

42 m

6.

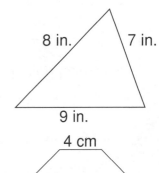

8 in.   7 in.

9 in.

7.

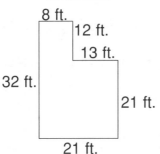

8 ft.

12 ft.

13 ft.

32 ft.

21 ft.

21 ft.

8.

4 cm

Math Grade 5—RBP0040

Robin and her friends are working for a landscaping company. Help them find the answer to each question. Remember to write the unit of measurement in your answer.

1. Robin is building a backyard fence. Two of the sides are 43 feet, and the other two sides are 57 feet. How much fencing does Robin need?

2. Eric is making a square flower bed in his yard. What is the perimeter of his flower bed if each edge measures 259 inches?

3. Marcy is roping off an area for a vegetable garden. Her garden measures 38 feet by 69 feet. How many feet of rope will Marcy need to buy?

4. Doug is putting a lawn border around the edge of the yard. The yard measures 76 feet by 83 feet. How many feet of border will he need to put down?

5. Robin is putting tile around the edge of a swimming pool. Her swimming pool measures 40 feet by 35 feet. How many feet of tile will Robin have to put down?

6. Rachel is making a planter box. If her box measures 345 inches long and 543 inches wide, how many inches of board will she need?

Find the area of each object.

ReMemBeR... To find the **area** of a rectangular figure, multiply the length by the width. Write your answer in or by the figure.

1.

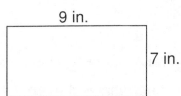

9 in.

7 in.

2.

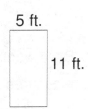

5 ft.

11 ft.

3.

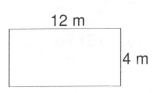

12 m

4 m

4.

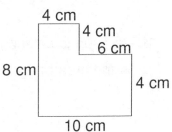

4 cm

4 cm

6 cm

8 cm

4 cm

10 cm

5.

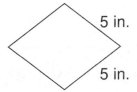

6 cm

4 cm

6.

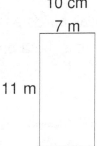

7 m

11 m

7.

5 in.

5 in.

8.

14 in.

5 in.

Solve each problem. Remember to write the unit of measurement in your answer.

1. Mitch measures the bedroom for new carpet. The room measures 14 feet by 27 feet. How much carpet will he need?

2. Belle wants to put new glass in her window. If her window
measures 34 inches by 48 inches, what is the area of the glass
she will need?

3. Jackson is painting his wall. The wall is 10 feet by 23 feet. What
is the area of the wall?

4. Lucas builds a table that is 86 inches wide and 92 inches long.
What is the area of his table?

5. Anna makes a quilt for her bed. If the quilt measures 90 inches
by 108 inches, what is the area of her quilt?

6. Bob builds a shed in his backyard. If the shed measures 56
meters by 83 meters, what is the area of his shed?

Solve each problem.

1. ^{2}64   87   17   92
           x 7   x 3   x 6   x 5
         448

2.   771   365   204   880
           x 2   x 6   x 3   x 7

3.   6,479   5,478   1,367   2,247
          x   9   x   8   x   4   x   3

4. Leslie typed 4 articles for her magazine. If each article had 1,432 words, how many words did she type altogether?

5. Carlos proofread 7 stories for his magazine. If each story had 304 paragraphs, how many paragraphs did Carlos proofread altogether?

6. Jamie read 8 magazines. If each magazine had 124 pages, how many pages did Jamie read altogether?

Solve each problem.

1.
$$\begin{array}{r} 93 \\ \times\ 3 \end{array}$$
$$\begin{array}{r} 76 \\ \times\ 2 \end{array}$$
$$\begin{array}{r} 23 \\ \times\ 9 \end{array}$$
$$\begin{array}{r} 49 \\ \times\ 5 \end{array}$$

2.
$$\begin{array}{r} 856 \\ \times\ 7 \end{array}$$
$$\begin{array}{r} 963 \\ \times\ 4 \end{array}$$
$$\begin{array}{r} 116 \\ \times\ 2 \end{array}$$
$$\begin{array}{r} 905 \\ \times\ 6 \end{array}$$

3.
$$\begin{array}{r} 8,824 \\ \times\ 8 \end{array}$$
$$\begin{array}{r} 4,653 \\ \times\ 3 \end{array}$$
$$\begin{array}{r} 2,749 \\ \times\ 7 \end{array}$$
$$\begin{array}{r} 5,556 \\ \times\ 9 \end{array}$$

4. Marcus bought 4 packages of nails. If each package contained 751 nails, how many nails did Marcus buy altogether?

5. A package of staples has 1,245 staples. If Lucy has 5 packages, how many staples does she have altogether?

6. The hardware store sold 3 crates of hammers. If each crate contained 16 hammers, how many hammers did they sell altogether?

18

1 tablespoon = 3 teaspoons
1 pint = 2 cups
1 quart = 2 pints
1 gallon = 4 quarts
1 pound = 16 ounces

Draw a line to the equivalent measurement.

1. 27 teaspoons   12 pints

2. 6 quarts   32 cups

3. 32 ounces   5 pints

4. 16 pints   6 tablespoons

5. 10 cups   2 pounds

6. 18 teaspoons   9 tablespoons

Solve each problem.

7. Gwen is making pancakes for her friends. If her recipe calls for 9 teaspoons of sugar, how many tablespoons should she use?

8. Scott is making grape juice. If he has 2 quarts, how many 1-cup servings can he pour?

9. If Abby has 1 gallon of syrup, how many pints does she have?

Vacation Time

> 1 year = 12 months
> 24 hours = 1 day
> 7 days = 1 week
> 60 minutes = 1 hour

Draw a line to the equivalent measurement.

1. 48 hours   240 minutes

2. 49 days   28 days

3. 3 years   7 weeks

4. 4 hours   36 months

5. 180 minutes   2 days

6. 4 weeks   3 hours

Solve each problem.

7. Emily went on vacation for 21 days. How many weeks was she gone on vacation?

8. Randy's flight was 150 minutes. How many hours did he spend flying?

9. Gary spent 5 weeks hiking and backpacking on his vacation. How many days was he gone on vacation?

20

Write the missing answers.

1. 6 x 9 = _____

2. 36 ÷ 4 = _____

3. 4 = 16 ÷ _____

4. 5 = _____ ÷ 6

5. 2 = 24 ÷ _____

6. 7 = _____ ÷ 9

7. _____ = 49 ÷ 7

8. _____ = 144 ÷ 12

9. 3 = 21 ÷ _____

10. _____ = 72 ÷ 9

11. 20 = _____ x 4

12. 5 x _____ = 25

13. _____ = 44 ÷ 11

14. 81 = _____ x 9

15. 8 x _____ = 32

16. 28 = 7 x _____

17. 15 ÷ 3 = _____

18. 6 x 4 = _____

19. 30 ÷ 5 = _____

20. 3 = 18 ÷ _____

21. 6 = _____ ÷ 8

22. 2 = 20 ÷ _____

23. 6 = _____ ÷ 2

24. _____ = 84 ÷ 7

25. _____ = 14 ÷ 2

26. _____ = 6 ÷ 3

27. 24 = _____ x 8

28. 5 x _____ = 25

29. _____ = 40 ÷ 5

30. 88 = _____ x 8

31. _____ = 45 ÷ 9

32. 64 = _____ x 8

Math Grade 5—RBP0040

Solve each problem. Draw a line to match the problem with the correct answer.

1.   64
      x 4

74

2.   24
      x 7

2,940

3.   96
      x 5

256

4.   37
      x 2

5,682

5.   68
      x 8

3,976

6. 735
     x 4

168

7. 947
     x 6

544

8. 568
     x 7

480

Solve each problem.

1.
$$\begin{array}{r} \overset{2}{8}7 \\ \times\ 41 \\ \hline 87 \\ +\ 3480 \\ \hline \mathbf{3{,}567} \end{array}$$

$$\begin{array}{r} 58 \\ \times\ 27 \\ \hline \end{array}$$

$$\begin{array}{r} 45 \\ \times\ 16 \\ \hline \end{array}$$

$$\begin{array}{r} 90 \\ \times\ 23 \\ \hline \end{array}$$

2.
$$\begin{array}{r} 71 \\ \times\ 22 \\ \hline \end{array}$$

$$\begin{array}{r} 85 \\ \times\ 86 \\ \hline \end{array}$$

$$\begin{array}{r} 17 \\ \times\ 53 \\ \hline \end{array}$$

$$\begin{array}{r} 37 \\ \times\ 97 \\ \hline \end{array}$$

3.
$$\begin{array}{r} 26 \\ \times\ 49 \\ \hline \end{array}$$

$$\begin{array}{r} 34 \\ \times\ 76 \\ \hline \end{array}$$

$$\begin{array}{r} 65 \\ \times\ 25 \\ \hline \end{array}$$

$$\begin{array}{r} 18 \\ \times\ 24 \\ \hline \end{array}$$

4.
$$\begin{array}{r} 72 \\ \times\ 64 \\ \hline \end{array}$$

$$\begin{array}{r} 43 \\ \times\ 39 \\ \hline \end{array}$$

$$\begin{array}{r} 92 \\ \times\ 72 \\ \hline \end{array}$$

$$\begin{array}{r} 65 \\ \times\ 12 \\ \hline \end{array}$$

Find the Quotient

Solve each problem and find the quotient.

1. $3\overline{)\,57}$ **19**
$$\begin{array}{r} 19 \\ 3\overline{)\,57} \\ -3 \\ \hline 27 \end{array}$$

2. $7\overline{)\,182}$

3. $8\overline{)\,336}$

4. $6\overline{)\,558}$

5. $2\overline{)\,98}$

6. $5\overline{)\,140}$

7. $3\overline{)\,252}$

8. $9\overline{)\,459}$

9. $4\overline{)\,268}$

10. $5\overline{)\,325}$

11. $2\overline{)\,78}$

12. $4\overline{)\,396}$

13. $2\overline{)\,166}$

14. $6\overline{)\,276}$

15. $4\overline{)\,324}$

Find the quotient.

1. $\overset{\textbf{17}\text{R1}}{5\overline{)86}}$
$\underline{-5}$
36
$\underline{-35}$
1

2. $2\overline{)64}$

3. $8\overline{)14}$

4. $7\overline{)67}$

5. $6\overline{)85}$

6. $2\overline{)45}$

7. $4\overline{)70}$

8. $3\overline{)28}$

9. $9\overline{)75}$

10. $3\overline{)46}$

11. $8\overline{)95}$

12. $4\overline{)91}$

13. $3\overline{)54}$

14. $7\overline{)51}$

15. $6\overline{)45}$

Solve each problem.

1. $23\overline{)534}$

2. $64\overline{)831}$

3. $44\overline{)641}$

4. $10\overline{)968}$

5. $86\overline{)357}$

6. $42\overline{)118}$

7. $13\overline{)372}$

8. $57\overline{)754}$

9. $61\overline{)789}$

10. $72\overline{)904}$

11. $55\overline{)127}$

12. $11\overline{)809}$

Solve each problem.

1. 36) 866   **2.** 92) 491

3. 63) 431   **4.** 23) 762

5. 19) 298   **6.** 33) 318

7. 11) 626   **8.** 72) 984

9. 49) 597   **10.** 88) 978

11. 58) 125   **12.** 10) 907

          Math Grade 5—RBP0040

1. What time was it 2 hours and 30 minutes earlier?

_____

2. What time was it 1 hour and 15 minutes earlier?

_____

3. What time will it be in 4 hours and 30 minutes?

_____

4. What time was it 3 hours and 45 minutes earlier?

_____

5. Kevin got to school at 8:25 a.m. He was 15 minutes late. What time did school start?

6. Ruth left 35 minutes before her piano lesson. If her piano lesson was at 9:45 a.m., what time did she leave?

7. Stacy has 45 minutes left before the concert ends. It is 10:05 p.m. What time does the concert end?

8. Jasmine left the store at 10:15 a.m. and drove home in 25 minutes. What time did she arrive home?

From the statements below, draw the correct number of points on the graph.

Games Won

Bears _____

Panthers _____

Bulldogs _____

🟡 = 4 games

1. The Bears won 24 games.

2. The Panthers won half as many games as the Bears.

3. The Bulldogs won 16 games.

4. How many more games did the Bears win than the Bulldogs?

Points Scored

Bears   Panthers

🟡 = 10 points

🔸 = 5 points

5. Which team scored the most points?

6. How many points did the Panthers score?

7. How many points did the Bears score?

8. How many more points did the Bears score than the Panthers?

29

Nicole's class took a poll of the fifth graders at her school to see what type of pets students have. Use the circle graph below to answer the questions.

Fifth Graders' Pets

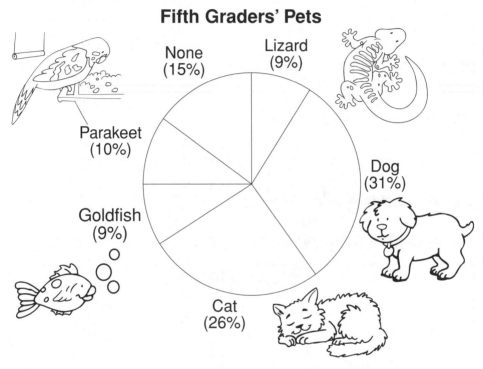

1. What percent of students have a cat?

2. What is the most popular pet?

3. What percent of students don't have a pet?

4. How many students have a pet with feathers?

5. Which two pets do the same percent of students have?

6. What's the total percent of students that have pets with fur?

30

Write the fraction for each picture.

1.

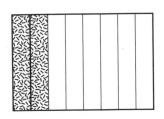

2.

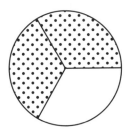

3.

4.

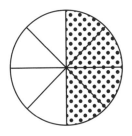

5.

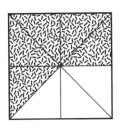

6.

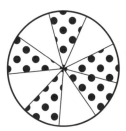

7.

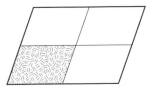

8.

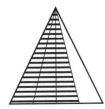

9.

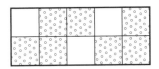

Math Grade 5—RBP0040

Shade the parts that show the fraction.

1.

$\frac{1}{2} =$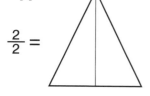

2.

$\frac{3}{8} =$

3.

$\frac{3}{2} =$

4.

$\frac{5}{8} =$

5.

$\frac{2}{4} =$

6.

$\frac{6}{12} =$

7.

$\frac{2}{2} =$

8.

$\frac{4}{16} =$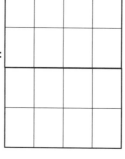

9.

$\frac{1}{4} =$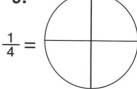

Janice is recording the distance each member of the track team ran. Help her change each score to a mixed number.

1. John $\frac{59}{8}$ miles = _____

2. Keshia $\frac{14}{3}$ miles = _____

3. Caroline $\frac{37}{7}$ miles = _____

4. Gary $\frac{26}{2}$ miles = _____

5. Jenny $\frac{35}{6}$ miles = _____

6. Mitch $\frac{11}{5}$ miles = _____

Rewrite the fraction as a mixed number.

7. $\frac{92}{11}$ =

8. $\frac{17}{4}$ =

9. $\frac{64}{10}$ =

10. $\frac{37}{5}$ =

11. $\frac{43}{6}$ =

12. $\frac{25}{2}$ =

13. $\frac{41}{8}$ =

14. $\frac{27}{3}$ =

15. $\frac{51}{7}$ =

16. $\frac{77}{9}$ =

17. $\frac{67}{8}$ =

18. $\frac{83}{9}$ =

Circle the equivalent fractions.

1. $\frac{7}{10}$ = $\frac{1}{4}$ $\boxed{\frac{14}{20}}$ $\frac{3}{21}$ $\boxed{\frac{21}{30}}$ $\frac{14}{10}$

2. $\frac{3}{8}$ = $\frac{1}{8}$ $\frac{3}{16}$ $\frac{6}{16}$ $\frac{9}{16}$ $\frac{9}{24}$

3. $\frac{1}{2}$ = $\frac{2}{4}$ $\frac{3}{4}$ $\frac{4}{8}$ $\frac{4}{16}$ $\frac{10}{20}$

4. $\frac{2}{3}$ = $\frac{1}{3}$ $\frac{2}{6}$ $\frac{4}{6}$ $\frac{4}{12}$ $\frac{6}{9}$

5. $\frac{2}{5}$ = $\frac{4}{10}$ $\frac{4}{25}$ $\frac{4}{5}$ $\frac{6}{15}$ $\frac{8}{20}$

6. $\frac{1}{8}$ = $\frac{4}{8}$ $\frac{2}{16}$ $\frac{3}{16}$ $\frac{3}{24}$ $\frac{4}{32}$

7. $\frac{1}{4}$ = $\frac{2}{4}$ $\frac{2}{5}$ $\frac{6}{12}$ $\frac{2}{8}$ $\frac{3}{12}$

8. $\frac{1}{6}$ = $\frac{1}{12}$ $\frac{2}{6}$ $\frac{2}{12}$ $\frac{3}{18}$ $\frac{3}{36}$

Fill in the missing number.

9. $\frac{1}{3} = \frac{5}{\bigcirc}$

10. $\frac{2}{\bigcirc} = \frac{4}{18}$

11. $\frac{5}{8} = \frac{\bigcirc}{40}$

12. $\frac{1}{4} = \frac{9}{\bigcirc}$

13. $\frac{\bigcirc}{5} = \frac{3}{15}$

14. $\frac{2}{11} = \frac{\bigcirc}{66}$

Fill in the missing number to complete the equivalent fraction.

1. $\frac{1}{9} = \frac{5}{\bigcirc}$

2. $\frac{2}{11} = \frac{8}{\bigcirc}$

3. $\frac{\bigcirc}{2} = \frac{8}{16}$

4. $\frac{1}{4} = \frac{\bigcirc}{32}$

5. $\frac{4}{16} = \frac{1}{\bigcirc}$

6. $\frac{2}{3} = \frac{24}{\bigcirc}$

7. $\frac{1}{\bigcirc} = \frac{3}{27}$

8. $\frac{5}{\bigcirc} = \frac{25}{30}$

9. $\frac{18}{45} = \frac{2}{\bigcirc}$

10. $\frac{2}{1} = \frac{24}{\bigcirc}$

11. $\frac{\bigcirc}{7} = \frac{18}{63}$

12. $\frac{6}{\bigcirc} = \frac{12}{14}$

Write each fraction in the lowest terms.

13. $\frac{12}{16} =$

14. $\frac{12}{144} =$

15. $\frac{25}{45} =$

16. $\frac{32}{40} =$

17. $\frac{18}{42} =$

18. $\frac{8}{88} =$

Rewrite each fraction as a mixed number.

1. $\frac{14}{3} = 4\frac{2}{3}$

2. $\frac{16}{5} =$

3. $\frac{13}{5} =$

4. $\frac{9}{8} =$

5. $\frac{13}{8} =$

6. $\frac{21}{6} =$

7. $\frac{19}{3} =$

8. $\frac{7}{5} =$

9. $\frac{10}{4} =$

10. $\frac{11}{5} =$

11. $\frac{8}{7} =$

12. $\frac{12}{5} =$

13. $\frac{15}{7} =$

14. $\frac{19}{17} =$

15. $\frac{16}{5} =$

Solve each problem. Rewrite your answer as a mixed number.

16. Sam walks 8/10 of a mile each way to work. What is the total number of miles he walks to and from work each day?

17. Lexi biked 7/8 of a mile to the concert. Then she biked 5/8 of a mile with her friend. How far did she bike altogether?

Working Backwards

Work backwards and change each mixed number into an improper fraction.

1. $4\frac{2}{3} =$

2. $3\frac{1}{5} =$

3. $6\frac{1}{3} =$

4. $1\frac{3}{4} =$

5. $2\frac{7}{8} =$

6. $1\frac{1}{2} =$

7. $5\frac{1}{5} =$

8. $2\frac{3}{5} =$

9. $2\frac{5}{8} =$

10. $7\frac{2}{3} =$

11. $4\frac{3}{4} =$

12. $3\frac{1}{3} =$

13. $6\frac{1}{2} =$

14. $1\frac{5}{8} =$

15. $3\frac{2}{3} =$

16. $4\frac{5}{6} =$

17. $1\frac{7}{16} =$

18. $1\frac{11}{12} =$

19. $4\frac{5}{8} =$

20. $6\frac{1}{3} =$

Write the fraction that goes with each picture.

1.

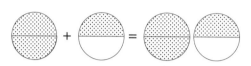

$$\underline{\quad 1 \quad} + \underline{\frac{1}{2}} = \underline{1\frac{1}{2}}$$

2.

$$\underline{\hspace{2cm}} + \underline{\hspace{2cm}} = \underline{\hspace{2cm}}$$

3.

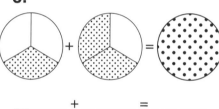

$$\underline{\hspace{2cm}} + \underline{\hspace{2cm}} = \underline{\hspace{2cm}}$$

4.

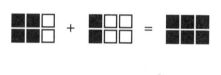

$$\underline{\hspace{2cm}} + \underline{\hspace{2cm}} = \underline{\hspace{2cm}}$$

5.

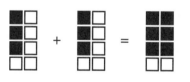

$$\underline{\hspace{2cm}} + \underline{\hspace{2cm}} = \underline{\hspace{2cm}}$$

6.

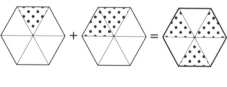

$$\underline{\hspace{2cm}} + \underline{\hspace{2cm}} = \underline{\hspace{2cm}}$$

7.

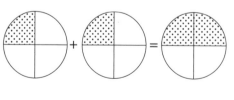

$$\underline{\hspace{2cm}} + \underline{\hspace{2cm}} = \underline{\hspace{2cm}}$$

8.

$$\underline{\hspace{2cm}} + \underline{\hspace{2cm}} = \underline{\hspace{2cm}}$$

Write the fraction that goes with each picture.

1.

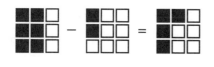

_____ – _____ = _____

2.

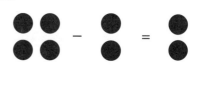

_____ – _____ = _____

3.

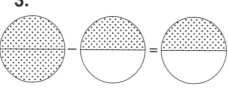

_____ – _____ = _____

4.

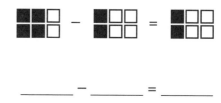

_____ – _____ = _____

5.

_____ – _____ = _____

6.

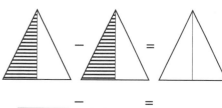

_____ – _____ = _____

7.

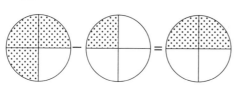

_____ – _____ = _____

8.

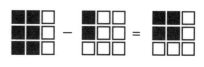

_____ – _____ = _____

Math Grade 5—RBP0040

Solve each problem. Remember to write your answers in simplest terms and change improper fractions to mixed numbers.

1. $\dfrac{5}{4}$
   $+\dfrac{2}{4}$
   $\dfrac{7}{4} = 1\dfrac{3}{4}$

2. $\dfrac{7}{8}$
   $+\dfrac{3}{8}$

3. $\dfrac{9}{14}$
   $-\dfrac{2}{14}$

4. $\dfrac{6}{7}$
   $-\dfrac{1}{7}$

5. $\dfrac{3}{16}$
   $+\dfrac{5}{16}$

6. $\dfrac{7}{3}$
   $+\dfrac{4}{3}$

7. $\dfrac{10}{9}$
   $-\dfrac{7}{9}$

8. $\dfrac{4}{5}$
   $+\dfrac{5}{5}$

9. $\dfrac{11}{12}$
   $-\dfrac{6}{12}$

10. $\dfrac{27}{13}$
    $-\dfrac{16}{13}$

11. $\dfrac{2}{6}$
    $+\dfrac{9}{6}$

12. $\dfrac{10}{8}$
    $+\dfrac{7}{8}$

13. $\dfrac{2}{3}$
    $\dfrac{8}{3}$
    $+\dfrac{5}{3}$

14. $\dfrac{7}{11}$
    $\dfrac{3}{11}$
    $+\dfrac{4}{11}$

15. $\dfrac{21}{2}$
    $\dfrac{13}{2}$
    $+\dfrac{3}{2}$

Write the fraction that goes with each picture.

1.

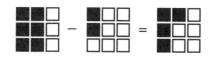

_____ – _____ = _____

2.

_____ – _____ = _____

3.

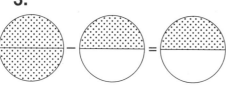

_____ – _____ = _____

4.

_____ – _____ = _____

5.

_____ – _____ = _____

6.

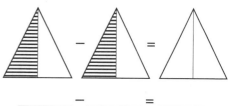

_____ – _____ = _____

7.

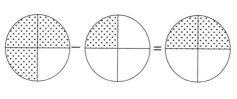

_____ – _____ = _____

8.

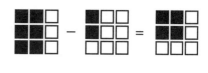

_____ – _____ = _____

Math Grade 5—RBP0040

Solve each problem. Remember to write your answers in simplest terms and change improper fractions to mixed numbers.

1.
$$\frac{5}{4}$$
$$+\ \frac{2}{4}$$
$$\frac{7}{4} = 1\frac{3}{4}$$

2.
$$\frac{7}{8}$$
$$+\ \frac{3}{8}$$

3.
$$\frac{9}{14}$$
$$-\ \frac{2}{14}$$

4.
$$\frac{6}{7}$$
$$-\ \frac{1}{7}$$

5.
$$\frac{3}{16}$$
$$+\ \frac{5}{16}$$

6.
$$\frac{7}{3}$$
$$+\ \frac{4}{3}$$

7.
$$\frac{10}{9}$$
$$-\ \frac{7}{9}$$

8.
$$\frac{4}{5}$$
$$+\ \frac{5}{5}$$

9.
$$\frac{11}{12}$$
$$-\ \frac{6}{12}$$

10.
$$\frac{27}{13}$$
$$-\ \frac{16}{13}$$

11.
$$\frac{2}{6}$$
$$+\ \frac{9}{6}$$

12.
$$\frac{10}{8}$$
$$+\ \frac{7}{8}$$

13.
$$\frac{2}{3}$$
$$\frac{8}{3}$$
$$+\ \frac{5}{3}$$

14.
$$\frac{7}{11}$$
$$\frac{3}{11}$$
$$+\ \frac{4}{11}$$

15.
$$\frac{21}{2}$$
$$\frac{13}{2}$$
$$+\ \frac{3}{2}$$

Find the Fraction

Circle the equivalent fractions.

1. $\frac{7}{10} =$ $\frac{1}{4}$ $\boxed{\frac{14}{20}}$ $\frac{3}{21}$ $\boxed{\frac{21}{30}}$ $\frac{14}{10}$

2. $\frac{3}{8} =$ $\frac{1}{8}$ $\frac{3}{16}$ $\frac{6}{16}$ $\frac{9}{16}$ $\frac{9}{24}$

3. $\frac{1}{2} =$ $\frac{2}{4}$ $\frac{3}{4}$ $\frac{4}{8}$ $\frac{4}{16}$ $\frac{10}{20}$

4. $\frac{2}{3} =$ $\frac{1}{3}$ $\frac{2}{6}$ $\frac{4}{6}$ $\frac{4}{12}$ $\frac{6}{9}$

5. $\frac{2}{5} =$ $\frac{4}{10}$ $\frac{4}{25}$ $\frac{4}{5}$ $\frac{6}{15}$ $\frac{8}{20}$

6. $\frac{1}{8} =$ $\frac{4}{8}$ $\frac{2}{16}$ $\frac{3}{16}$ $\frac{3}{24}$ $\frac{4}{32}$

7. $\frac{1}{4} =$ $\frac{2}{4}$ $\frac{2}{5}$ $\frac{6}{12}$ $\frac{2}{8}$ $\frac{3}{12}$

8. $\frac{1}{6} =$ $\frac{1}{12}$ $\frac{2}{6}$ $\frac{2}{12}$ $\frac{3}{18}$ $\frac{3}{36}$

Fill in the missing number.

9. $\frac{1}{3} = \frac{5}{\bigcirc}$

10. $\frac{2}{\bigcirc} = \frac{4}{18}$

11. $\frac{5}{8} = \frac{\bigcirc}{40}$

12. $\frac{1}{4} = \frac{9}{\bigcirc}$

13. $\frac{\bigcirc}{5} = \frac{3}{15}$

14. $\frac{2}{11} = \frac{\bigcirc}{66}$

Fill in the missing number to complete the equivalent fraction.

1. $\frac{1}{9} = \frac{5}{\bigcirc}$

2. $\frac{2}{11} = \frac{8}{\bigcirc}$

3. $\frac{\bigcirc}{2} = \frac{8}{16}$

4. $\frac{1}{4} = \frac{\bigcirc}{32}$

5. $\frac{4}{16} = \frac{1}{\bigcirc}$

6. $\frac{2}{3} = \frac{24}{\bigcirc}$

7. $\frac{1}{\bigcirc} = \frac{3}{27}$

8. $\frac{5}{\bigcirc} = \frac{25}{30}$

9. $\frac{18}{45} = \frac{2}{\bigcirc}$

10. $\frac{2}{1} = \frac{24}{\bigcirc}$

11. $\frac{\bigcirc}{7} = \frac{18}{63}$

12. $\frac{6}{\bigcirc} = \frac{12}{14}$

Write each fraction in the lowest terms.

13. $\frac{12}{16} =$

14. $\frac{12}{144} =$

15. $\frac{25}{45} =$

16. $\frac{32}{40} =$

17. $\frac{18}{42} =$

18. $\frac{8}{88} =$

Rewrite each fraction as a mixed number.

1. $\frac{14}{3} = \mathbf{4\frac{2}{3}}$

2. $\frac{16}{5} =$

3. $\frac{13}{5} =$

4. $\frac{9}{8} =$

5. $\frac{13}{8} =$

6. $\frac{21}{6} =$

7. $\frac{19}{3} =$

8. $\frac{7}{5} =$

9. $\frac{10}{4} =$

10. $\frac{11}{5} =$

11. $\frac{8}{7} =$

12. $\frac{12}{5} =$

13. $\frac{15}{7} =$

14. $\frac{19}{17} =$

15. $\frac{16}{5} =$

Solve each problem. Rewrite your answer as a mixed number.

16. Sam walks 8/10 of a mile each way to work. What is the total number of miles he walks to and from work each day?

17. Lexi biked 7/8 of a mile to the concert. Then she biked 5/8 of a mile with her friend. How far did she bike altogether?

Janice is recording the distance each member of the track team ran. Help her change each score to a mixed number.

1. John $\frac{59}{8}$ miles = _____

2. Keshia $\frac{14}{3}$ miles = _____

3. Caroline $\frac{37}{7}$ miles = _____

4. Gary $\frac{26}{2}$ miles = _____

5. Jenny $\frac{35}{6}$ miles = _____

6. Mitch $\frac{11}{5}$ miles = _____

Rewrite the fraction as a mixed number.

7. $\frac{92}{11}$ =   **8.** $\frac{17}{4}$ =   **9.** $\frac{64}{10}$ =

10. $\frac{37}{5}$ =   **11.** $\frac{43}{6}$ =   **12.** $\frac{25}{2}$ =

13. $\frac{41}{8}$ =   **14.** $\frac{27}{3}$ =   **15.** $\frac{51}{7}$ =

16. $\frac{77}{9}$ =   **17.** $\frac{67}{8}$ =   **18.** $\frac{83}{9}$ =

Work backwards and change each mixed number into an improper fraction.

1. $4\frac{2}{3} =$

2. $3\frac{1}{5} =$

3. $6\frac{1}{3} =$

4. $1\frac{3}{4} =$

5. $2\frac{7}{8} =$

6. $1\frac{1}{2} =$

7. $5\frac{1}{5} =$

8. $2\frac{3}{5} =$

9. $2\frac{5}{8} =$

10. $7\frac{2}{3} =$

11. $4\frac{3}{4} =$

12. $3\frac{1}{3} =$

13. $6\frac{1}{2} =$

14. $1\frac{5}{8} =$

15. $3\frac{2}{3} =$

16. $4\frac{5}{6} =$

17. $1\frac{7}{16} =$

18. $1\frac{11}{12} =$

19. $4\frac{5}{8} =$

20. $6\frac{1}{3} =$

Math Grade 5—RBP0040

Write the fraction that goes with each picture.

1.

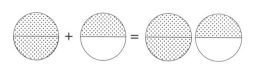

$$\underline{\quad 1 \quad} + \underline{\frac{1}{2}} = \underline{1\frac{1}{2}}$$

2.

$$\underline{\qquad} + \underline{\qquad} = \underline{\qquad}$$

3.

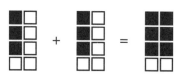

$$\underline{\qquad} + \underline{\qquad} = \underline{\qquad}$$

4.

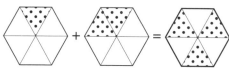

$$\underline{\qquad} + \underline{\qquad} = \underline{\qquad}$$

5.

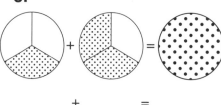

$$\underline{\qquad} + \underline{\qquad} = \underline{\qquad}$$

6.

$$\underline{\qquad} + \underline{\qquad} = \underline{\qquad}$$

7.

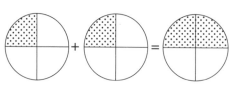

$$\underline{\qquad} + \underline{\qquad} = \underline{\qquad}$$

8.

$$\underline{\qquad} + \underline{\qquad} = \underline{\qquad}$$

Find the lowest common denominator; then add or subtract the
fractions. Write your answers in simplest terms and rewrite
improper fractions as mixed numbers.

1. $\dfrac{3}{2} = \dfrac{6}{4}$

$+ \dfrac{3}{4} = + \dfrac{3}{4}$

$\dfrac{9}{4} = 2\dfrac{1}{4}$

2. $\dfrac{3}{8} = \underline{\quad}$

$+ \dfrac{3}{16} = + \underline{\quad}$

3. $\dfrac{6}{2} = \underline{\quad}$

$+ \dfrac{5}{6} = + \underline{\quad}$

4. $\dfrac{20}{10} = \underline{\quad}$

$- \dfrac{7}{20} = - \underline{\quad}$

5. $\dfrac{9}{8} = \underline{\quad}$

$+ \dfrac{5}{2} = - \underline{\quad}$

6. $\dfrac{6}{4} = \underline{\quad}$

$- \dfrac{2}{6} = - \underline{\quad}$

Find the lowest common denominator; then add or subtract the fractions. Write your answers in simplest terms and rewrite improper fractions as mixed numbers.

1. $\dfrac{2}{9}$ = _____

$\dfrac{5}{6}$ = _____

+ _____ +_____

2. $\dfrac{6}{7}$ = _____

$-\dfrac{2}{14}$ = _____

− _____

3. $\dfrac{4}{2}$ = _____

$\dfrac{7}{8}$ = _____

+ _____ +_____

4. $\dfrac{11}{4}$ = _____

$\dfrac{4}{5}$ = _____

+ _____ +_____

5. $\dfrac{2}{11}$ = _____

$-\dfrac{4}{55}$ = _____

− _____

6. $\dfrac{9}{6}$ = _____

$-\dfrac{7}{8}$ = _____

− _____

Find the lowest common denominator; then add or subtract the fractions. Write your answers in simplest terms and rewrite improper fractions as mixed numbers.

1. $\dfrac{3}{2} = \dfrac{6}{4}$

$+ \dfrac{3}{4} = + \dfrac{3}{4}$

$\dfrac{9}{4} = 2\dfrac{1}{4}$

2. $\dfrac{3}{8} = \underline{\quad}$

$+ \dfrac{3}{16} = + \underline{\quad}$

3. $\dfrac{6}{2} = \underline{\quad}$

$+ \dfrac{5}{6} = + \underline{\quad}$

4. $\dfrac{20}{10} = \underline{\quad}$

$- \dfrac{7}{20} = - \underline{\quad}$

5. $\dfrac{9}{8} = \underline{\quad}$

$+ \dfrac{5}{2} = - \underline{\quad}$

6. $\dfrac{6}{4} = \underline{\quad}$

$- \dfrac{2}{6} = - \underline{\quad}$

Find the lowest common denominator; then add or subtract the fractions. Write your answers in simplest terms and rewrite improper fractions as mixed numbers.

1. $\frac{2}{9}$ = ____

   $\frac{5}{6}$ = ____

   $+$ ___ $+$ ____

2. $\frac{6}{7}$ = ____

   $-\frac{2}{14}$ = $-$ ____

3. $\frac{4}{2}$ = ____

   $\frac{7}{8}$ = ____

   $+$ ___ $+$ ____

4. $\frac{11}{4}$ = ____

   $\frac{4}{5}$ = ____

   $+$ ___ $+$ ____

5. $\frac{2}{11}$ = ____

   $-\frac{4}{55}$ = $-$ ____

6. $\frac{9}{6}$ = ____

   $-\frac{7}{8}$ = $-$ ____

First, rewrite each mixed number as an improper fraction. Then find the lowest common denominator and add or subtract the fractions. Write your answers in simplest terms and rewrite improper fractions as mixed numbers.

1. $3\frac{1}{3} =$ ⬚

$+\ 2\frac{5}{6} =$ ⬚

2. $8\frac{2}{4} =$ ⬚

$-\ 2\frac{2}{3} =$ ⬚

3. $1\frac{1}{9} =$ ⬚

$+\ 4\frac{7}{3} =$ ⬚

4. $5\frac{1}{4} =$ ⬚

$+\ 2\frac{1}{2} =$ ⬚

5. $3\frac{2}{5} =$ ⬚

$-\ 1\frac{4}{5} =$ ⬚

6. $7\frac{5}{8} =$ ⬚

$-\ 2\frac{1}{6} =$ ⬚

Solve each problem. Remember to write your answers in simplest terms and rewrite improper fractions as mixed numbers.

1. Jason used $\frac{2}{3}$ yard of string for his kite. Then he used another $\frac{5}{8}$ yard. How many yards of string did Jason use altogether?

2. Katie bought 2 yards of fabric for her project. She used $\frac{1}{3}$ yard of fabric. How many yards of fabric did she have left?

3. Doris measured $\frac{3}{8}$ yard of ribbon. Then she measured $\frac{2}{3}$ yard more. How many yards of ribbon did she measure altogether?

4. Curtis bought a piece of wood that measured $7\frac{1}{3}$ feet. He cut off a piece that measured $1\frac{5}{8}$ feet. How long is the piece he has left?

5. Allison bought $5\frac{2}{3}$ yards of trim for her quilt. Then she bought another $3\frac{7}{8}$ yards. How many yards of trim did she buy altogether?

6. Melissa bought $2\frac{1}{3}$ yards of yarn for her project. She used $\frac{3}{4}$ yard. How many yards of yarn did she have left?

44

First, rewrite each mixed number as an improper fraction. Then find the lowest common denominator and add or subtract the fractions. Write your answers in simplest terms and rewrite improper fractions as mixed numbers.

1. $3\frac{1}{3} =$ $\boxed{\dfrac{\quad}{\quad}}$

$+ \ 2\frac{5}{6} =$ $+ \dfrac{\quad}{\quad}$

2. $8\frac{2}{4} =$ $\boxed{\dfrac{\quad}{\quad}}$

$- \ 2\frac{2}{3} =$ $- \dfrac{\quad}{\quad}$

3. $1\frac{1}{9} =$ $\boxed{\dfrac{\quad}{\quad}}$

$+ \ 4\frac{7}{3} =$ $+ \dfrac{\quad}{\quad}$

4. $5\frac{1}{4} =$ $\boxed{\dfrac{\quad}{\quad}}$

$+ \ 2\frac{1}{2} =$ $+ \dfrac{\quad}{\quad}$

5. $3\frac{2}{5} =$ $\boxed{\dfrac{\quad}{\quad}}$

$- \ 1\frac{4}{5} =$ $- \dfrac{\quad}{\quad}$

6. $7\frac{5}{8} =$ $\boxed{\dfrac{\quad}{\quad}}$

$- \ 2\frac{1}{6} =$ $- \dfrac{\quad}{\quad}$

Solve each problem. Remember to write your answers in simplest terms and rewrite improper fractions as mixed numbers.

1. Jason used $\frac{2}{3}$ yard of string for his kite. Then he used another $\frac{5}{8}$ yard. How many yards of string did Jason use altogether?

2. Katie bought 2 yards of fabric for her project. She used $\frac{1}{3}$ yard of fabric. How many yards of fabric did she have left?

3. Doris measured $\frac{3}{8}$ yard of ribbon. Then she measured $\frac{2}{3}$ yard more. How many yards of ribbon did she measure altogether?

4. Curtis bought a piece of wood that measured $7\frac{1}{3}$ feet. He cut off a piece that measured $1\frac{5}{8}$ feet. How long is the piece he has left?

5. Allison bought $5\frac{2}{3}$ yards of trim for her quilt. Then she bought another $3\frac{7}{8}$ yards. How many yards of trim did she buy altogether?

6. Melissa bought $2\frac{1}{3}$ yards of yarn for her project. She used $\frac{3}{4}$ yard. How many yards of yarn did she have left?

44

Write the decimal for each fraction.

1. $\frac{5}{100}$ = __.05__

4. $\frac{84}{1000}$ = _____

7. $\frac{7}{10}$ = _____

2. $\frac{7}{1000}$ = _____

5. $\frac{7}{100}$ = _____

8. $\frac{15}{100}$ = _____

3. $\frac{92}{100}$ = _____

6. $\frac{43}{1000}$ = _____

9. $\frac{9}{10}$ = _____

Write the fraction for each decimal.

10. .075 = _____

13. .021 = _____

16. .09 = _____

11. .03 = _____

14. .04 = _____

17. .11 = _____

12. .086 = _____

15. .21 = _____

18. .005 = _____

Write the percent for each decimal.

19. .08 = _____

22. .72 = _____

25. .62 = _____

20. .19 = _____

23. .33 = _____

26. .07 = _____

21. .21 = _____

24. .98 = _____

27. .04 = _____

Write the missing fraction, decimal, or percent in the chart below. The first one is done for you.

	Fraction	Decimal	Percent
1.	$\frac{5}{100}$	.05	5%
2.			14%
3.	$\frac{27}{100}$		
4.			32%
5.		.89	
6.			57%
7.	$\frac{9}{100}$		
8.		.17	
9.	$\frac{71}{100}$		
10.			43%
11.		.34	
12.	$\frac{64}{100}$		
13.		.75	

Math Grade 5—RBP0040

Solve each problem. Remember to write the unit of measurement in your answers.

1. Heidi and Lisa are making cookies. Their recipe calls for $\frac{3}{4}$ cup of oatmeal. If they triple their recipe, how many cups of oatmeal will they need?

2. Justin and Nicole use $\frac{2}{3}$ yard of string on their kite. If they make 7 kites, how many yards of string will they need?

3. Krista and Webster use $\frac{5}{8}$ of a package of paper for their report. If they make 9 reports, how many packages of paper will they need?

4. Lance and Maria use $\frac{7}{8}$ cup of laundry detergent for 1 load of laundry. If they wash 7 loads of laundry, how many cups of detergent do they need?

5. Marcy and Anna use $1\frac{2}{3}$ cups of sugar in their jam recipe. If they make 4 batches, how many cups of sugar will they need?

6. Rob and Thomas use $4\frac{1}{3}$ bottles of motor oil on a car. If they put oil in 9 cars, how many bottles of motor oil will they need to buy?

Multiply each problem. Then rewrite your answer in simplest terms.

RememBeR... To multiply a fraction, first multiply the numerator by the numerator and then multiply the denominator by the denominator.

Example: $\frac{1}{4} \times \frac{2}{3} = \frac{2}{12} = \frac{1}{6}$

1. $\frac{3}{4} \times \frac{2}{5} =$

2. $\frac{6}{7} \times \frac{7}{8} =$

3. $\frac{1}{2} \times 10 =$

4. $5 \times \frac{5}{8} =$

5. $\frac{1}{3} \times \frac{4}{5} =$

6. $\frac{1}{6} \times \frac{2}{3} =$

7. $\frac{4}{5} \times \frac{1}{6} =$

8. $\frac{7}{8} \times \frac{3}{4} =$

9. $7 \times \frac{1}{8} =$

10. $\frac{8}{9} \times \frac{2}{5} =$

Write the missing numbers for the decimal values in the chart below.

	tenths	hundredths	thousandths
1. four-hundredths	0	4	
2. six-thousandths			
3. thirty-six thousandths			
4. ten-hundredths			
5. twenty-seven thousandths			
6. ninety-two hundredths			
7. forty-seven thousandths			
8. eighty-nine hundredths			
9. two-tenths			
10. eight-hundredths			

Write the decimal number for each problem.

1. 3 and 6 tenths

5. 6 and 1 hundredth

2. 1 and 8 hundredths

6. 8 and 2 hundredths

3. 7 and 2 tenths

7. 3 and 32 thousandths

4. 4 and 2 thousandths

8. 9 and 7 tenths

Write the decimal number.

9. $108 \frac{7}{10} =$ _____ **13.** $64 \frac{2}{100} =$ _____ **17.** $82 \frac{5}{100} =$ _____

10. $34 \frac{4}{100} =$ _____ **14.** $216 \frac{3}{10} =$ _____ **18.** $16 \frac{7}{10} =$ _____

11. $56 \frac{93}{100} =$ _____ **15.** $81 \frac{5}{10} =$ _____ **19.** $38 \frac{5}{10} =$ _____

12. $20 \frac{9}{100} =$ _____ **16.** $42 \frac{9}{1000} =$ _____ **20.** $11 \frac{27}{100} =$ _____

9. $108 \frac{7}{10}$ = _____

13. $64 \frac{2}{100}$ = _____

17. $82 \frac{5}{100}$ = _____

10. $34 \frac{4}{100}$ = _____

14. $216 \frac{3}{10}$ = _____

18. $16 \frac{7}{10}$ = _____

11. $56 \frac{93}{100}$ = _____

15. $81 \frac{5}{10}$ = _____

19. $38 \frac{5}{10}$ = _____

12. $20 \frac{9}{100}$ = _____

16. $42 \frac{9}{1000}$ = _____

20. $11 \frac{27}{100}$ = _____

Round each number to the nearest tenth.

1. 2.07 __**2.1**__   **2.** 5.67 _____   **3.** 7.38 _____

5.42 _____   33.01 _____   8.61 _____

7.39 _____   68.96 _____   4.97 _____

26.55 _____   122.18 _____   80.83 _____

Round each number to the nearest hundredth.

4. 3.047 _____   **5.** 9.921 _____   **6.** 8.043 _____

62.686 _____   4.769 _____   27.977 _____

1.588 _____   5.815 _____   3.251 _____

51.971 _____   81.745 _____   6.378 _____

Round each number to the nearest tenth.

1. 4.58 _____   **2.** 19.96 _____   **3.** 8.16 _____

12.87 _____   20.08 _____   9.42 _____

Round each number to the nearest hundredth.

4. 6.877 _____   **5.** 4.058 _____   **6.** 97.470 _____

8.876 _____   87.069 _____   1.387 _____

Round each number to the nearest thousandth.

7. 1.0649 _____   **8.** 93.0129 ____   **9.** 7.2199 _____

22.5240 _____   51.8490 ____   3.7672 _____

Put the correct sign (>, <, =) in each problem.

1. .007 $\boxed{<}$ .07

10. .08 ◯ .8

2. 2.159 ◯ 2.259

11. 101.05 ◯ 101.005

3. 10.05 ◯ 10.005

12. 9.50 ◯ 7.05

4. 0.99 ◯ .009

13. 214.01 ◯ 214.001

5. 30.249 ◯ 30.429

14. 9.008 ◯ 9.08

6. .004 ◯ 4.00

15. 614.05 ◯ 614.05

7. 6.041 ◯ 6.401

16. 8.26 ◯ 8.026

8. 92.001 ◯ 92.001

17. 43.014 ◯ 43.104

9. 263.08 ◯ 263.81

18. .83 ◯ .63

Math Grade 5—RBP0040

Put the prices on the menu in order from least to greatest.

$1.25 $2.03 $1.07 $2.51 $1.10 $2.15 $2.21 $1.05

Item:	Price:
Soda	
Milk	
Fries	
Salad	
Cheese Sandwich	
Tuna Sandwich	
Hamburger	
Cheeseburger	

Circle the largest decimal number in each row.

1. 4.05   4.50   4.005   4.15

2. 10.57   10.49   10.005   10.057

3. 2.5   2.15   2.52   2.005

4. 1.8   1.84   1.48   1.847

5. 89.90   88.19   8.90   89.09

Solve each problem. Write the letter from the box on the line below that matches the answer.

A 64.42 + 6.70	**C** 57.10 + 43.99	**T** 248.80 − 57.98
H 100.3 − 78.87	**E** 123.50 + 64.75	
E 454.6 − 56.8	**H** 84.96 + 86.75	

This is the fastest land animal, with a speed of approximately 70 miles per hour.

101.09	21.43	188.25	397.8	190.82	71.12	171.71

Solve each problem. Write the letter from the box on the line below that matches the answer.

R	G	A
917.42 + 32.70	52.10 − 33.76	566.50 + 512.65
O 207.4 − 67.57	**D** 75.100 + 75.867	**N** 257.30 + 65.82
F 267.50 − 176.88	**Y** 798.52 + 357.90	**L** 9.008 − 8.789

This is the fastest insect, with a speed of approximately 35 miles per hour.

___ ___ ___ ___ ___ ___ ___ ___ ___
150.967 950.12 1,079.15 18.34 139.83 323.12 90.62 .219 1156.42

Decimal Delights

Solve each problem. Remember to write the decimal point in your answer.

1.
$$\overset{5\ 3}{2.64}$$
$$\underline{\times\ \ 9}$$
23.76

2.
6.48
$$\underline{\times\ \ 7}$$

3.
72.7
$$\underline{\times\ \ 8}$$

4.
12.9
$$\underline{\times\ 17}$$

5.
54.87
$$\underline{\times\ \ 24}$$

6.
97.02
$$\underline{\times\ 32}$$

7.
3.348
$$\underline{\times\ \ \ 63}$$

8.
4.05
$$\underline{\times\ 69}$$

9.
2.469
$$\underline{\times\ 236}$$

10.
6.009
$$\underline{\times\ \ 48}$$

11.
71.865
$$\underline{\times\ \ \ 45}$$

12.
98.077
$$\underline{\times\ \ \ 45}$$

Math Grade 5—RBP0040

Which Costs More?

Use the price list to solve each problem. Remember to write the decimal point in your answer.

Item	Price per Pound
apples	$0.97
bananas	$0.56
peaches	$0.72
pears	$0.84
plums	$0.65
oranges	$0.33
grapes	$1.09

1. Anne buys 3 pounds of bananas. Meg buys 5 pounds of apples. Who spends more, Anne or Meg?

2. James buys 6 pounds of peaches. How much does James spend on peaches?

3. If Susan buys 4 pounds of oranges and 3 pounds of pears, which fruit does she spend the most money on, oranges or pears?

4. Mason buys 9 pounds of grapes. His sister buys 10 pounds of apples. Who spends more, Mason or his sister?

5. Travis buys 7 pounds of pears. Lisa buys 8 pounds of peaches. Who spends more, Travis or Lisa?

6. Jesse buys 5 pounds of oranges and 4 pounds of bananas. What does she spend the most money on, oranges or bananas?

Megan's class voted on their favorite Winter Olympic events. Use the circle graph to answer the questions.

Favorite Winter Olympic Events

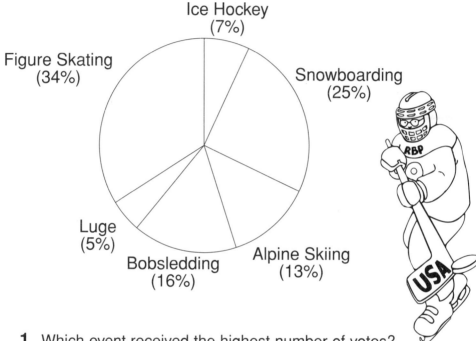

1. Which event received the highest number of votes?

2. What percent of students voted for bobsledding?

3. Which event did 34% of the students vote for as their favorite?

4. What was the total percentage of students that liked the luge and bobsledding altogether?

5. How many more students voted for snowboarding than alpine skiing?

Math Grade 5—RBP0040

On-the-Dot Division

Solve each problem. Remember to write the decimal point in your answer.

1.
$$\begin{array}{r} \mathbf{4.25} \\ 6\overline{)\,25.50} \\ \underline{24} \\ 15 \\ \underline{12} \\ 30 \\ \underline{30} \\ 0 \end{array}$$

2. $7\overline{)\,3.99}$

3. $3\overline{)\,83.7}$

4. $3\overline{)\,19.05}$

5. $7\overline{)\,11.62}$

6. $4\overline{)\,49.12}$

7. $8\overline{)\,1.96}$

8. $7\overline{)\,55.86}$

9. $2\overline{)\,12.62}$

10. $4\overline{)\,3.04}$

11. $2\overline{)\,1.826}$

12. $9\overline{)\,5.526}$

The Spin It music store is looking at their CD sales during the past months. Use the line graph to answer the questions.

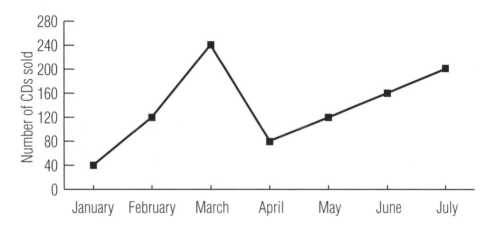

Spin It CD Sales

1. In what month were the most CDs sold?

2. In which 2 months were the same number of CDs sold?

3. How many CDs were sold in May?

4. What happened to the number of sales during the months of April through May?

5. How many more CDs were sold in March than in April?

6. What was the average number of CDs sold during January through April?

Roberto kept track of the amount of rainfall at his school for three months. Use the bar graph to answer the questions.

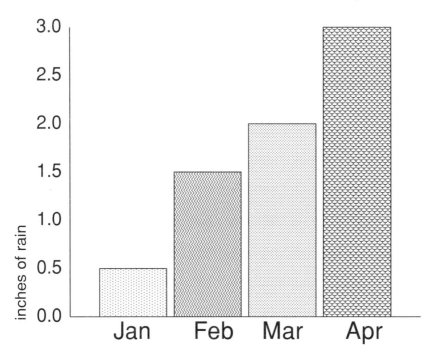

Rainfall at Roosevelt Elementary

1. Which month had the most rain?

2. Which month had the least rain?

3. How many more inches did it rain in April than in March?

4. In which month did Roosevelt get 2 inches of rain?

5. What was the average amount of rain for January through April?

Olympic Medals

Remember...

- The **range** is the difference between the highest number and the lowest number in the data.
- To calculate the **mean** (or average), add the list of numbers and then divide by the number of items.
- The **median** is the middle number that appears in the data.
- The **mode** is the number that appears most often in the data.

The 2000 Summer Olympic Games were held in Sydney, Australia. Use the chart to answer the questions about the number of medals awarded at the games.

Country	Number of Medals
United States	97
Russia	88
China	59
Australia	58
Germany	57
France	38
Italy	34
Cuba	29
Britain	28
South Korea	28
Romania	26

1. What is the range of the data?

2. What is the mode of the data?

3. What is the median of the data?

4. What is the average number of medals awarded?

Math Grade 5—RBP0040

Leslie kept track of her math test scores:

```
100
95
85
83
82
82
76
```

1. What is the range of her test scores?

2. What is the mode of her test scores?

3. What is the median of her test scores?

4. What is the mean of her test scores? Round your answer.

Paulo also kept track of his test scores:

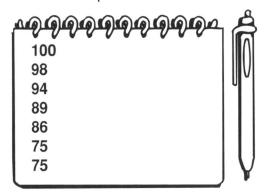

```
100
98
94
89
86
75
75
```

5. What is the range of his test scores?

6. What is the mode of his test scores?

7. What is the median of his test scores?

8. What is the mean of his test scores? Round your answer.

Bookworm Buddies

Figure out the number of pages each book club member read. Fill in the table to help organize the information.

Caroline read 5 times as many pages as Max.

Julie read 346 pages more than Greg.

Max read half as many pages as Allison.

Greg read 1,598 pages less than Caroline.

Allison read 2,424 pages.

Becky read 2 times as many pages as Greg.

Name:	Pages Read:

Math Grade 5—RBP0040

Bookworm Buddies

Solve each problem using the information in the table from the previous page.

1. Who read the most pages?

2. How many more pages did Caroline read than Julie?

3. What was the average number of pages read? Round your answer.

4. How many pages did Max and Becky read altogether?

5. If Max read 2 books and each book had the same number of pages, how many pages did each book have?

6. If Julie reads 2 pages in 1 minute, how many minutes did it take her to read all of her pages?

At the Zoo

Use the information to draw a map of the city zoo in the space below.

1. Key: 1/2 inch = 12 yards on the map

2. The lion house is 72 yards east of the zoo's entrance.

3. The elephant habitat is 36 yards south of the lion house.

4. The reptile house is 72 yards west of the elephant habitat.

5. The butterfly house is 36 yards east of the reptile house.

6. The penguin exhibit is 18 yards north of the butterfly house.

Entrance

Math Grade 5—RBP0040

At the Zoo

Use the information on your map of the zoo to answer the questions.

1. Jeremy walked from the zoo entrance to the lion house. Then he walked to the elephant habitat. How far did Jeremy walk altogether?

2. What is the shortest distance from the zoo's entrance to the reptile house?

3. Simon looked at lizards and butterflies. Rachael looked at the lions and snakes. Who walked farther, Simon or Rachael?

4. How many yards is it from the penguin exhibit to the butterfly house?

5. How much farther is it from the zoo entrance to the elephant habitat than from the butterfly house to the penguin exhibit?

6. What is the area of the part of the zoo that shows on the map?

Mall Mania

Stuart and his friends went to the mall. Use the prices on the items to solve these problems.

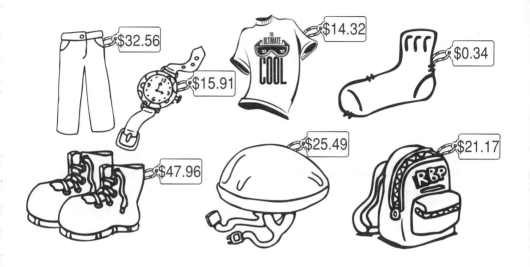

1. Stuart buys a pair of boots and a pair of jeans. How much does Stuart spend altogether?

2. Paula has $45.00. She buys a bike helmet and a watch. How much does she have left?

3. Jan spends $8.84 on socks. How many socks does she buy?

Mall Mania

Stuart and his friends went to the mall. Use the prices on the items to solve these problems.

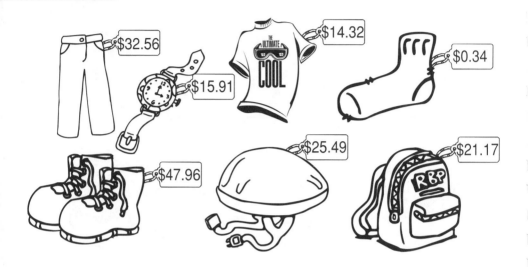

1. Rick's aunt gave him $60.00 for his birthday. He buys a pair of boots. Does he have enough money left over to buy a pair of jeans?

2. Marcy buys 2 watches and a backpack. How much does she spend altogether?

3. Scott spends $57.28 on T-shirts. How many T-shirts does he buy?

Dessert Delights

Carmen is baking cakes for her school's carnival. She needs to bring 168 pieces of cake. If each cake can be cut into 12 servings, how many cakes will Carmen need to make?

Help Carmen convert her cake recipe so she will have enough servings.

Carmen's Chocolate Cake Recipe:

2 1/4 cups flour   _____

1 3/4 cups sugar   _____

1/2 cup cocoa   _____

1 1/8 teaspoons baking soda   _____

2 1/4 tablespoons butter   _____

1 3/8 cups milk   _____

2 1/4 teaspoons vanilla   _____

1 egg   _____

Math Grade 5—RBP0040

Dessert Delights

1. Les brings an apple pie and a blueberry pie to the carnival. He cuts each pie into 8 pieces. Three people eat a piece of apple pie, and 6 people eat a piece of blueberry pie. If Les combines the leftover pieces in a pie tin, what fraction of a whole pie does he have left?

2. Martin makes 324 cookies. He puts 1 dozen cookies in each package. How many packages does he end up with?

3. At the carnival, 7 people bring 2 dozen cookies each. How many cookies are there altogether?

4. Jan has 4 quarts of ice cream. How many 1-cup servings can she scoop?

5. Dylan is frosting cupcakes. If he frosts 13 cupcakes with 1 package of frosting, how many packages of frosting does he need to frost 117 cupcakes?

Answer Pages

Page 1

Alabama	52,000	52,400
Alaska	663,000	663,300
California	164,000	163,700
Delaware	2,000	2,500
Georgia	59,000	59,400
Kansas	82,000	82,300
Maryland	12,000	12,400
Mississippi	48,000	48,400
Nevada	111,000	110,600
New York	55,000	54,600
Oregon	98,000	98,400
Rhode Island	2,000	1,500
Texas	269,000	268,600
Wyoming	98,000	97,800

Page 2

1. 52,576   **2.** 26,915   **3.** 38,515
4. 434,629   **5.** 968,331   **6.** 660,182
7. 933,507   **8.** 306,132   **9.** 711,361
10. 457,229   **11.** 203,874

Page 3

1. 731   **2.** 34,730   **3.** 60,273
4. 264   **5.** 27,694   **6.** 16,792
7. 89,463   **8.** 589   **9.** 36,835
10. 230,589   **11.** 465

Page 4

1.	725	1,699	1,374	592
2.	5,424	10,895	11,661	13,173
3.	111,246	130,430	110,920	98,510
4.	1,561	710	1,871	1,815
5.	19,454	15,701	22,113	18,740

Page 5

1.	7,685	10,918	9,818	5,726
2.	105,124	56,237	84,873	69,119
3.	980,774	170,781	577,687	715,363
4.	1,110,044	1,061,592	1,847,386	1,310,895
5.	19,553	28,325	14,853	22,444

Page 6

1. >   **2.** <   **3.** >   **4.** >   **5.** >
6. >   **7.** =   **8.** <   **9.** >   **10.** <
11. <   **12.** <   **13.** =   **14.** >   **15.** >
16. >   **17.** <   **18.** =

Page 7

1.	367	151	69	516
2.	34	108	387	265
3.	685	286	169	155
4.	1,594	4,168	163	4,175
5.	2,582	1,304	4,608	6,885

Page 8

1.	497	156	202	207
2.	287	188	479	379
3.	79	604	228	680
4.	2,494	2,356	4,646	4,688
5.	56,197	84,096	13,096	51,712

Page 9

1. $1 + $3 + $3 + $4 + $2 = $13.00
2. $2 + $2 + $2 + $3 + $1 = $10.00
3. $1 + $3 + $8 = $12.00
4. $3 + $3 + $3 + $4 + $4 + $4 + $4 = $25.00
5. $2 + $4 + $4 + $4 = $14.00
6. $1 + $1 + $8 + $2 = $12.00
7. $2 + $2 + $2 + $1 + $1 = $8.00
8. $3 + $3 + $3 + $8 = $17.00

Page 10

1. $12.39   **2.** $9.99   **3.** $11.58   **4.** $25.23
5. $14.94   **6.** $11.77   **7.** $9.01   **8.** $15.35

Page 11

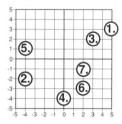

8. (-1, -3)   **9.** (2, -2)   **10.** (3, 2)
11. (1, 1)   **12.** (-2, -1)   **13.** (-3, 2)

Math Grade 5—RBP0040

Answer Pages

Page 12

1. (2, 2) **2.** (2, -1) **3.** (-2, -2)
4. (-4, 3) **5.** (4, 1) **6.** (3, -3)

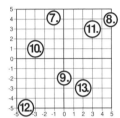

Page 13

1. 48 m **2.** 35 m **3.** 36 in. **4.** 74 cm
5. 110 m **6.** 24 in. **7.** 107 ft. **8.** 32 cm

Page 14

1. 200 feet of fencing **2.** 1,036 inches
3. 214 feet of rope **4.** 318 feet of lawn
5. 150 feet of tile **6.** 1,776" of board

Page 15

1. 63 sq. in. **2.** 55 sq. ft. **3.** 48 sq. m
4. 56 sq. cm **5.** 24 sq. cm **6.** 77 sq. m
7. 25 sq. in. **8.** 70 sq. in.

Page 16

1. 378 sq. feet **2.** 1,632 sq. inches
3. 230 sq. feet **4.** 7,912 sq. inches
5. 9,720 sq. inches **6.** 4,648 sq. meters

Page 17

1. 448 261 102 460
2. 1,542 2,190 612 6,160
3. 58,311 43,824 5,468 6,741
4. 5,728 words
5. 2,128 paragraphs
6. 992 pages

Page 18

1. 279 152 207 245
2. 5,992 3,852 232 5,430
3. 70,592 13,959 19,243 50,004
4. 3,004 nails
5. 6,225 staples
6. 48 hammers

Page 19

1. 9 tablespoons **2.** 12 pints **3.** 2 pounds
4. 32 cups **5.** 5 pints **6.** 6 tablespoons
7. 3 tablespoons **8.** 8 cups **9.** 8 pints

Page 20

1. 2 days **2.** 7 weeks **3.** 36 months
4. 240 minutes **5.** 3 hours **6.** 28 days
7. 3 weeks **8.** $2\frac{1}{2}$ hours **9.** 35 days

Page 21

1. 54 **2.** 9 **3.** 4 **4.** 30 **5.** 12
6. 63 **7.** 7 **8.** 12 **9.** 7 **10.** 8
11. 5 **12.** 5 **13.** 4 **14.** 9 **15.** 4
16. 4 **17.** 5 **18.** 24 **19.** 6 **20.** 6
21. 48 **22.** 10 **23.** 12 **24.** 12 **25.** 7
26. 2 **27.** 3 **28.** 5 **29.** 8 **30.** 11
31. 5 **32.** 8

Page 22

1. 256 **2.** 168 **3.** 480 **4.** 74
5. 544 **6.** 2,940 **7.** 5,682 **8.** 3,976

Page 23

1. 3,567 1,566 720 2,070
2. 1,562 7,310 901 3,589
3. 1,274 2,584 1,625 432
4. 4,608 1,677 6,624 780

Page 24

1. 19 **2.** 26 **3.** 42 **4.** 93 **5.** 49
6. 28 **7.** 84 **8.** 51 **9.** 67 **10.** 65
11. 39 **12.** 99 **13.** 83 **14.** 46 **15.** 81

Page 25

1. 17 R1 **2.** 32 **3.** 1 R6 **4.** 9 R4
5. 14 R1 **6.** 22 R1 **7.** 17 R2 **8.** 9 R1
9. 8 R3 **10.** 15 R1 **11.** 11 R7 **12.** 22 R3
13. 18 **14.** 7 R2 **15.** 7 R3

Page 26

1. 23 R5 **2.** 12 R63 **3.** 14 R25
4. 96 R8 **5.** 4 R13 **6.** 2 R34
7. 28 R8 **8.** 13 R13 **9.** 12 R57
10. 12 R40 **11.** 2 R17 **12.** 73 R6

Answer Pages

Page 27
1. 24 R2 2. 5 R31 3. 6 R53 4. 33 R3
5. 15 R13 6. 9 R21 7. 56 R10 8. 13 R48
9. 12 R9 10. 11 R10 11. 2 R9 12. 90 R7

Page 28
1. 2:30 2. 8:15 3. 6:30 4. 3:00
5. 8:10 6. 9:10 7. 10:50 8. 10:40

Page 29

Games Won	
Bears	_ _ _
Panthers	_ _ _ _ _ _ _ _ _
Bulldogs	_ _ _ _ _ _
	= 4 games

4. 8 games 5. the Bears 6. 65 points
7. 75 points 8. 10 points

Page 30
1. 26 percent   2. dog
3. 15 percent   4. 10 percent
5. lizard and goldfish   6. 57 percent

Page 31
1. $\frac{2}{8}$ 2. $\frac{2}{3}$ 3. $\frac{1}{6}$ 4. $\frac{4}{8}$ 5. $\frac{5}{8}$
6. $\frac{5}{9}$ 7. $\frac{1}{4}$ 8. $\frac{3}{4}$ 9. $\frac{7}{10}$

Page 32
1.   2.

3.   4.

5.   6.

7.   8.

9.

Page 33
1. $\frac{14}{20}, \frac{21}{30}$ 2. $\frac{6}{16}, \frac{9}{24}$ 3. $\frac{2}{4}, \frac{4}{8}, \frac{10}{20}$ 4. $\frac{4}{6}, \frac{6}{9}$
5. $\frac{4}{10}, \frac{6}{15}, \frac{8}{20}$ 6. $\frac{2}{16}, \frac{3}{24}, \frac{4}{32}$ 7. $\frac{2}{8}, \frac{3}{12}$ 8. $\frac{2}{12}, \frac{3}{18}$
9. 15 10. 9 11. 25 12. 36 13. 1 14. 12

Page 34
1. 45 2. 44 3. 1 4. 8 5. 4 6. 36
7. 9 8. 6 9. 5 10. 12 11. 2 12. 7
13. $\frac{3}{4}$ 14. $\frac{1}{12}$ 15. $\frac{5}{9}$ 16. $\frac{4}{5}$ 17. $\frac{3}{7}$ 18. $\frac{1}{11}$

Page 35
1. $4\frac{2}{3}$ 2. $3\frac{1}{5}$ 3. $2\frac{3}{5}$
4. $1\frac{1}{8}$ 5. $1\frac{5}{8}$ 6. $3\frac{3}{6}$ or $3\frac{1}{2}$
7. $6\frac{1}{3}$ 8. $1\frac{2}{5}$ 9. $2\frac{2}{4}$ or $2\frac{1}{2}$
10. $2\frac{1}{5}$ 11. $1\frac{1}{7}$ 12. $2\frac{2}{5}$
13. $2\frac{1}{7}$ 14. $1\frac{2}{17}$ 15. $3\frac{1}{5}$
16. $1\frac{6}{10}$ or $1\frac{3}{5}$ miles   17. $1\frac{4}{8}$ or $1\frac{1}{2}$ miles

Page 36
1. $7\frac{3}{8}$ 2. $4\frac{2}{3}$ 3. $5\frac{2}{7}$ 4. 13 5. $5\frac{5}{6}$
6. $2\frac{1}{5}$ 7. $8\frac{4}{11}$ 8. $4\frac{1}{4}$ 9. $6\frac{4}{10}$ or $6\frac{2}{5}$
10. $7\frac{2}{5}$ 11. $7\frac{1}{6}$ 12. $12\frac{1}{2}$ 13. $5\frac{1}{8}$ 14. 9
15. $7\frac{2}{7}$ 16. $8\frac{5}{9}$ 17. $8\frac{3}{8}$ 18. $9\frac{2}{9}$

Page 37
1. $\frac{14}{3}$ 2. $\frac{16}{5}$ 3. $\frac{19}{3}$ 4. $\frac{7}{4}$ 5. $\frac{23}{8}$
6. $\frac{3}{2}$ 7. $\frac{26}{5}$ 8. $\frac{13}{5}$ 9. $\frac{21}{4}$ 10. $\frac{23}{3}$
11. $\frac{19}{4}$ 12. $\frac{10}{3}$ 13. $\frac{13}{2}$ 14. $\frac{13}{3}$ 15. $\frac{11}{3}$
16. $\frac{29}{6}$ 17. $\frac{23}{16}$ 18. $\frac{23}{12}$ 19. $\frac{37}{8}$ 20. $\frac{19}{3}$

Page 38
1. $\frac{2}{2} + \frac{1}{2} = \frac{3}{2}$ or $1\frac{1}{2}$ 2. $\frac{2}{4} + \frac{1}{4} = \frac{3}{4}$
3. $\frac{1}{3} + \frac{2}{3} = \frac{3}{3}$ or 1   4. $\frac{4}{6} + \frac{2}{6} = \frac{6}{6}$ or 1
5. $\frac{3}{8} + \frac{3}{8} = \frac{6}{8}$ or $\frac{3}{4}$ 6. $\frac{1}{6} + \frac{2}{6} = \frac{3}{6}$ or $\frac{1}{2}$
7. $\frac{1}{4} + \frac{1}{4} = \frac{2}{4}$ or $\frac{1}{2}$ 8. $\frac{3}{9} + \frac{2}{9} = \frac{5}{9}$

Page 39
1. $\frac{6}{9} - \frac{2}{9} = \frac{4}{9}$ 2. $\frac{4}{1} - \frac{1}{1} = \frac{2}{1}$ or 2
3. $\frac{2}{2} - \frac{1}{2} = \frac{1}{2}$ 4. $\frac{4}{6} - \frac{2}{6} = \frac{2}{6}$ or $\frac{1}{3}$
5. $\frac{3}{4} - \frac{2}{4} = \frac{1}{4}$ 6. $\frac{1}{2} - \frac{1}{2} = \frac{0}{2}$ or 0
7. $\frac{3}{4} - \frac{1}{4} = \frac{2}{4}$ or $\frac{1}{2}$ 8. $\frac{6}{9} - \frac{2}{9} = \frac{4}{9}$

Answer Pages

Page 40
1. $1\frac{3}{4}$ 2. $1\frac{1}{4}$ 3. $\frac{1}{2}$ 4. $\frac{5}{7}$ 5. $\frac{1}{2}$
6. $3\frac{2}{3}$ 7. $\frac{1}{3}$ 8. $1\frac{4}{5}$ 9. $\frac{5}{12}$ 10. $\frac{11}{13}$
11. $1\frac{5}{6}$ 12. $2\frac{1}{8}$ 13. 5 14. $1\frac{3}{11}$ 15. $18\frac{1}{2}$

Page 41
1. $2\frac{1}{4}$ 2. $\frac{9}{16}$ 3. $3\frac{5}{6}$ 4. $1\frac{13}{20}$ 5. $3\frac{5}{8}$ 6. $1\frac{1}{6}$

Page 42
1. $1\frac{1}{18}$ 2. $\frac{5}{7}$ 3. $2\frac{7}{8}$ 4. $3\frac{11}{20}$ 5. $\frac{6}{55}$ 6. $\frac{5}{8}$

Page 43
1. $6\frac{1}{6}$ 2. $5\frac{5}{6}$ 3. $7\frac{4}{9}$ 4. $7\frac{3}{4}$ 5. $1\frac{3}{5}$ 6. $5\frac{11}{24}$

Page 44
1. $1\frac{7}{24}$ yards 2. $1\frac{2}{3}$ yards 3. $1\frac{1}{24}$ yards
4. $5\frac{17}{24}$ feet 5. $9\frac{13}{24}$ yards 6. $1\frac{7}{12}$ yards

Page 45
1. $\frac{6}{20}$ or $\frac{3}{10}$ 2. $\frac{42}{56}$ or $\frac{3}{4}$ 3. $\frac{10}{2}$ or 5 4. $\frac{25}{7}$ or $3\frac{1}{8}$
5. $\frac{4}{15}$ 6. $\frac{2}{18}$ or $\frac{1}{9}$ 7. $\frac{4}{30}$ or $\frac{2}{15}$ 8. $\frac{21}{32}$
9. $\frac{7}{8}$ 10. $\frac{16}{45}$

Page 46
1. $2\frac{1}{4}$ cups 2. $4\frac{2}{3}$ yards 3. $5\frac{5}{8}$ packs
4. $6\frac{1}{8}$ cups 5. $6\frac{2}{3}$ cups 6. 39 bottles

Page 47
1. $\frac{5}{100}$ .05 5% 2. $\frac{14}{100}$ .14 14%
3. $\frac{27}{100}$ .27 27% 4. $\frac{32}{100}$ .32 32%
5. $\frac{89}{100}$ .89 89% 6. $\frac{57}{100}$ .57 57%
7. $\frac{9}{100}$ .09 9% 8. $\frac{17}{100}$ .17 17%
9. $\frac{71}{100}$ .71 71% 10. $\frac{43}{100}$ .43 43%
11. $\frac{34}{100}$ .34 34% 12. $\frac{64}{100}$ .64 64%
13. $\frac{75}{100}$ .75 75%

Page 48
1. .05 2. .007 3. .92 4. .084
5. .07 6. .043 7. .7 8. .15
9. .9 10. $\frac{75}{100}$ 11. $\frac{3}{100}$ 12. $\frac{86}{1000}$
13. $\frac{21}{1000}$ 14. $\frac{4}{100}$ 15. $\frac{21}{100}$ 16. $\frac{9}{100}$
17. $\frac{11}{100}$ 18. $\frac{5}{1000}$ 19. 8% 20. 19%
21. 21% 22. 72% 23. 33% 24. 98%
25. 62% 26. 7% 27. 4%

Page 49
1. .04 2. .006 3. .036 4. .10
5. .027 6. .92 7. .047 8. .89
9. .2 10. .08

Page 50
1. 3.6 2. 1.08 3. 7.2
4. 4.002 5. 6.01 6. 8.02
7. 3.032 8. 9.7 9. 108.7
10. 34.04 11. 56.93 12. 20.09
13. 64.02 14. 216.3 15. 81.5
16. 42.009 17. 82.05 18. 16.7
19. 38.5 20. 11.27

Page 51
1. 2.1 5.4 7.4 26.6
2. 5.7 33 69 122.2
3. 7.4 8.6 5 80.8
4. 3.05 62.69 1.59 51.97
5. 9.92 4.77 5.82 81.75
6. 8.04 27.98 3.25 6.38

Page 52
1. 4.6 12.9 2. 20.0 20.1
3. 8.2 9.4 4. 6.88 8.88
5. 4.06 87.07 6. 97.47 1.39
7. 1.065 22.524 8. 93.013 51.849
9. 7.220 3.767

Page 53
1. < 2. < 3. > 4. > 5. < 6. <
7. < 8. = 9. < 10. < 11. > 12. >
13. > 14. < 15. = 16. > 17. < 18. >

Page 54
$1.05 - $1.07 - $1.10 - $1.25
$2.03 - $2.15 - $2.21 - $2.51
1. 4.50 2. 10.57 3. 2.52
4. 1.847 5. 89.90

Page 55
cheetah

Page 56
dragonfly

Answer Pages

Page 57
1. 23.76   **2.** 45.36   **3.** 581.6
4. 219.3   **5.** 1,316.88   **6.** 3,104.64
7. 210.924   **8.** 279.45   **9.** 582.684
10. 288.432   **11.** 3,233.925   **12.** 4,413.465

Page 58
1. Meg   **2.** $4.32   **3.** pears
4. Mason   **5.** Travis   **6.** bananas

Page 59
1. figure skating   **2.** 16%
3. figure skating   **4.** 21%
5. 12%

Page 60
1. 4.25   **2.** .57   **3.** 27.9
4. 6.35   **5.** 1.66   **6.** 12.28
7. .245   **8.** 7.98   **9.** 6.31
10. .76   **11.** .913   **12.** .614

Page 61
1. March
2. February and May
3. 120
4. Sales went up, or increased.
5. 160 CDs
6. 120 CDs

Page 62
1. April
2. January
3. 1 inch
4. March
5. 1.75 inches

Page 63
1. 71
2. 28
3. 38
4. 49 medals

Page 64
1. 24   **2.** 82   **3.** 83   **4.** 86
5. 25   **6.** 75   **7.** 89   **8.** 88

Page 65
Allison   2,424
Max   1,212
Caroline   6,060
Greg   4,462
Becky   8,924
Julie   4,808

Page 66
1. Becky   **2.** 1,252 pages
3. 4,648 pages   **4.** 10,136 pages
5. 606 pages   **6.** 2,404 minutes

Page 68
1. 108 yards   **2.** 36 yards
3. Rachael   **4.** 18 yards
5. 90 yards   **6.** 2,592 sq. yards

Page 69
1. $80.52
2. $3.60
3. 26 pairs

Page 70
1. no
2. $52.99
3. 4

Page 71
74 Cakes
1. $31\frac{1}{2}$ cups   **2.** $24\frac{1}{2}$ cups
3. 7 cups   **4.** $15\frac{3}{4}$ tsp.
5. $31\frac{1}{2}$ tbsp.   **6.** $19\frac{1}{4}$ cups
7. $31\frac{1}{2}$ tsp.   **8.** 14 eggs

Page 72
1. $\frac{7}{8}$ of a pie
2. 27 packages
3. 168 cookies
4. 16 cups
5. 9 packages

Notes

Five things I'm thankful for:

1. _____
2. _____
3. _____
4. _____
5. _____